British Library Cataloguing in Publication Data

Moore, Clement C.
    The night before Christmas.
    I. Title   II. Stevenson, Peter, *1953*–
    813'.54 [J]   PZ7

    ISBN 0-340-33048-1

Illustrations copyright © Peter Stevenson 1983

First published 1983
Third impression 1986

Published by Hodder and Stoughton Children's Books,
a division of Hodder and Stoughton Ltd,
Mill Road, Dunton Green, Sevenoaks, Kent TN13 2YJ

Printed in Hong Kong

Designed by Graham Marks

The Night Before Christmas

Words
Clement C. Moore

Pictures
Peter Stevenson

HODDER AND STOUGHTON
LONDON SYDNEY AUCKLAND TORONTO

'Twas the night before Christmas,
when all through the house
Not a creature was stirring, not even
a mouse;
The stockings were hung by the
chimney with care,
In hopes that St Nicholas soon
would be there;

The children were nestled all snug in
    their beds
While visions of sugar-plums
    danced in their heads;
And mamma in her kerchief, and I in
    my cap,
Had just settled our brains for a long
    winter's nap, –

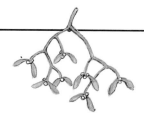

When out on the lawn there arose
  such a clatter,
I sprang from my bed to see what
  was the matter.
Away to the window I flew like a
  flash,
Tore open the shutters and threw up
  the sash.
The moon on the breast of the new-
  fallen snow
Gave a lustre of midday to objects
  below;
When what to my wondering eyes
  should appear,
But a miniature sleigh and eight tiny
  reindeer,

With a little old driver, so lively and
    quick,
I knew in a moment it must be St
    Nick.
More rapid than eagles his coursers
    they came,
And he whistled and shouted, and
    called them by name:
"Now, Dasher! now, Dancer! now,
    Prancer and Vixen!
On, Comet! on, Cupid! on, Donder
    and Blitzen!
To the top of the porch, to the top of
    the wall!
Now dash away, dash away, dash
    away, all!"

As dry leaves that before the wild
      hurricane fly,
When they meet with an obstacle,
      mount to the sky,

So up to the housetop the coursers
    they flew,
With the sleigh full of toys, and St
    Nicholas too.

And then in a twinkling I heard on
  the roof
The prancing and pawing of each
  little hoof.
As I drew in my head, and was
  turning around,
Down the chimney St Nicholas
  came with a bound.

He was dressed all in fur from his
    head to his foot,
And his clothes were all tarnished
    with ashes and soot;
A bundle of toys he had flung on his
    back,
And he looked like a peddler just
    opening a pack.
His eyes – how they twinkled! his
    dimples, how merry!
His cheeks were like roses, his nose
    like a cherry!
His droll little mouth was drawn up
    like a bow,
And the beard on his chin was as
    white as the snow.

The stump of a pipe he held tight in
    his teeth.
And the smoke it encircled his head
    like a wreath.
He had a broad face and a little
    round belly
That shook, when he laughed, like a
    bowl full of jelly.
He was chubby and plump, a right
    jolly old elf;
And I laughed when I saw him, in
    spite of myself.
A wink of his eye and a twist of his
    head
Soon gave me to know I had nothing
    to dread.

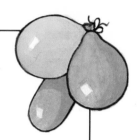

He spoke not a word, but went straight to his work,
And filled all the stockings; then turned with a jerk,
And laying his finger aside of his nose,
And giving a nod, up the chimney he rose.

He sprang to his sleigh, to his team
    gave a whistle,
And away they all flew like the down
    of a thistle;
But I heard him exclaim, ere he
    drove out of sight,
"Happy Christmas to all, and to all a
    good-night!"

Clement C. Moore